BROKEN

A Young Man's Search for Strength Through the Strings of Confinement
and Tragedy on a Dark Path to Freedom

Christopher Bolder

DEDICATION

To my grandmother Linda Stroud, who've always told me, no matter what I've been through good manners and respect will carry you through.

To my wife Brittney, who sacrifices are unmatched and love feels so unconditional.

I dedicate this book to you both

Table of Contents

ACKNOWLEDGMENTS

"I have to start by thanking my awesome wife, Brittney. From early advice to changing my rough drafts to giving me great feedback on my cover to keeping my little kiddos out my hair so I could edit and write, she was just as important to this book getting it done as I was. Thank you so much."

"I want to thank my dear Friend, Pastor and brother Cornelius Lindsey for his support and his encouragement that my story should be told, not only should it be told but that nations are waiting on my obedience and it will have the impact to influence lives to change and be transformed. Thank you I appreciate you believing in me."

"Writing a book is harder than I thought and more rewarding than. I could imagine have imagined. None of this would have been possible without my bravest heart my grandmother Linda H. Stroud. She is my backbone, she's stood by every challenge, struggle and any ounce of success I've endured. I love you mama"

'

CHAPTER 1
WHERE IT ALL WENT WRONG?

It was a cool and chilly night in November 2005. I was standing there in a stranger's backyard, as if I were their neighbor or friend who had been there before for a BBQ or game of horseshoes. Armed in a black ski mask and a black and white army camouflage jacket, and hands sweated under my gloves and tingled with numbness. But this was my first time in his backyard. This was my first time, a complete amateur at breaking & entering. My partner in crime, however, was excited as if he lived for this moment. I thought, 'Am I missing something? Was there another street code that I forgot?' Two African American males in broad daylight with hooded jackets and ski masks on, wasn't the norm in the parts I grew up in the rural areas of Kannapolis, North Carolina.

I paced back and forth, rehearsing the plan within conversation. I knew he could tell I was the dummy here, going in unarmed. As he paced holding his gun and rubbing his temple, my mind drifted... to a place where freedom had no limits. My adrenaline was bouncing off the walls. Fear pushed me. It pushed me up a flight of stairs and into the back door of this drug dealer's apartment.

CHAPTER 2
WHEN LIFE BEGAN

If you rewind the tape of my life to where it all started, you'll see a day compiled of broken pieces. I was born on January 12th, 1986, to a twelve-year-old mother.

"She's gone!!" shouted the nurse. "Oh, my God! She left! She left her son here in the hospital! She left her child!"

God has a way of bringing things around full effect. I remember a childhood story, told from the Bible: when Hannah prayed for a child because she was barren. After receiving a son, she named him Samuel-- only to leave him with the Prophet for her return home.

I had been abandoned and yet didn't even know it. I couldn't hear what was being said, I couldn't see what happened... but

God provided. My grandparents, John and Linda Stroud had come to see me that very day, after dealing with the turmoil of events that happened. They decided it was best that they keep me. After all, it was their daughter that had birthed and left me. The hospital was considering getting the state involved, but my grandmother was relentless. She was a fighter in seeing the right things get done, no matter who the person is. She's always been a fair and honest person and she did just that in making sure that didn't end up somewhere less fortunate. I could only imagine how my life would have shifted, having to grow up in foster care or being in an adoption system. Foster care would have mounted in visiting hours and court dates, an experience of frustration and timeless worries to get home to my biological family. Thank God for my grandparent's willingness to take me and care for me.

CHAPTER 3
THE GOOD OLE DAYS

Let's fast forward a second. I grew up in North Carolina in a small town called Kannapolis, a small mill town where everybody knew each other. Home of the legend NASCAR race driver Dale Earnhardt population of about 50,000 people. It is just north of the metro city of Charlotte. I grew up around a dysfunctional family. By the time I was nine years of age, 80% of my immediate family had all been incarcerated or had pending charges for felonies. In my world, if you didn't come from a wealthy or middle-class family, the only thing left for you to do was survive. If you didn't graduate, land a good job, or marry up, your survival rate and the chance at being successful were very low. The hood is a place where second chances aren't given out.

I had never met my dad and from what I was told about this time, he wasn't in a rush to meet me. I grew up wondering who my parents were and how I ended with my grandparents. The story was told to me many times, but only in anger or resentment that no one cared. I constantly wondered why. I felt the person telling me the story always played victim or was subconsciously crying out for help. And yet they told me they wanted me. I was a 'special child.' Their actions often showed differently.

My grandmother, who I call 'Mama' because she raised me, had two other children outside of marriage. To this day, I've never had a solid relationship with my biological mother's siblings. My Uncle Roderick, my mother's brother, has been serving time under a molestation charge for the past 22 years and currently still incarcerated under those charges. I have another uncle who is currently serving a life sentence for a rape charge and has been incarcerated for about 29 years. Quite a few of my immediate family has had a hard life, and I've watched my grandmother be there for them all.

Countless times, I watched my grandmother buying stamps to write letters to family and spending her Saturdays going from prison to prison. Mama invested more time in her incarcerated children than for herself. I lived with my grandparents since birth, and my mom would come around now and then, mostly when she wanted something. This went on for years; my grandmother disliked when she came around, but honestly it was a love hate relationship. The fact that she's around meant she's alive and not in jail, and on the other hand, she would steal something just about every time she came over to the house. But they let her in any way.

My grandparents were Pentecostal preachers. We were a very religious family. From what we watched on television and listened to on the radio, down to what we wore to church was very strict in our home. It was not like today's culture where it is alright to wear jeans with holes in them or to freely come to church as you feel, but we had to dress in suits, dress pants and button up shirts. Anything less gave the impression that you were a sinner someone who didn't have a relationship with God.

Because if you did it was assumed you knew better to dress the part. And yet church was charismatic and emotional , which is good, but I also felt a disconnect from our culture.

My biological mother was in and out of prison; she continued to struggle with drug addiction, prostitution, and other cycles of criminal activity to maintain her addictions. This left me feeling abandoned, hated, and rejected. I met my father for the first time at the age of 12. It was an awkward moment, at a high school basketball game in Kannapolis and a close friend of my dad's mentioned to me that my dad was there, walking me over to him as if the person knew I needed to be introduced. Yes, I was a bit intimidated. I mean, after all, this is the man that denied that I was his son. I recited the rumors in my head of what my family said, what he did and the accusations against him. But I still wondered the truth. And here I stood, two feet away, and all I could say was... "Hey," like a child that I was, too nervous to fight the past years of emotions. Something in me yelled, "Can you be here for me now?".

So, where did life start for me? How did I shape my identity? I'll be the first to tell you it wasn't easy. My grandparents were able to provide the basics of food and shelter, but financially it was difficult. The strain of having taken on to raise three grandchildren with low-income jobs and tough. My grandparents worked in the cotton mill plant 3rd shift for a number of years. Before long they decided to start delivering the daily newspaper for Independent Tribute in our hometown. This, of course, was in a day and time were people spent more time reading more than scrolling on their phones. My grandparents were workers, faithful church-goers, and pioneers within the community. As years past on, we got older, and the school system changed. When my grandparents were attending school in the 60's, and society was just ending segregation. But with my schooling, the time had changed and education had also changed. This meant they couldn't provide much support to me, educationally. , Soon, I was failing in school and it raised tension with me and my family.

I was raised to do two things: graduate from high school and land a job. My grandparents really thought and believed that working a "good job" would get me by. But times had changed. "They don't deliver milk anymore?!," they would ask.

I was tired of asking them for money only to hear, "Chris, we don't have it. It's tight right now, baby." I often went to school in need of a haircut, shoes, and new clothes. All I would hear from my grandparents was, "God will provide."

My grandfather had a side-hustle of fishing and picking up cans and scrap aluminum. He was the best fisherman I ever knew. He was so smooth. He could snag a fish out of your fish tank from our house. Countless times we had no food in the house and no funds to make ends meet, yet my grandfather managed to bring home a net full of fish. And so, we would eat fish for weeks at a time.

Growing up, I truly believed that "God would provide," until I was 15 years old and nothing was provided for, in my view. I felt like everything that we believed God to provide for us at times seemed like the opposite would happen. We trusted God yet ran in lack. One minute, the lights and power were cut off, and the next was when rent/mortgage payments were due. And still, I watched them tirelessly testify that God is good. They continued to preach the gospel, like there was no tomorrow and encouraging others in their faith, while our home was in chaos. I was losing what little faith I knew. After getting fired from my first job and having failing grades in school, my life drastically changed for the worst. I felt overwhelmed by a life that began with rejection and felt like I was constantly overlooked. I was desperate for someone to see me, to know me, to want me. I wanted my mother's love, but she was nowhere to be found; she was the neighborhood "crackhead." I wanted my dad to tell me, "You're going to make it, son." —And so, I turned from what I knew was right, and went down a dark path. I started hanging around the wrong crowd. I needed some type of peace. I didn't want to join a gang, but just wanted to be around a crew that had bond or brotherhood. I was looking for some sort of validation and belonging. Inside, I was screaming for help.

We were raised on the notion that you learned to play the hand that is dealt to you. In school I played football and was a decent fullback and middle linebacker. My determination of the sport was what made me a good player. My physique was good, but my ruthless nature at running the football was better. I could have had a shot at going to play college football. My passion for the game of football on the field was grandeur. And I was a good athletic in other baseball and basketball as well. Because I am ambidextrous, I proudly excelled in throwing a football with my left hand and throwing a baseball with my right. After getting expelled for skipping classes, having low failing grades, and getting into fights on school campus, I began to give up. I stopped caring and started dodging the church I was running from God and seeking another way out. Oh, God! No! The last place I wanted to be was in church. I would come in smelling like weed and the pastor would talk about me during his sermons in the state of mind I was in. What I received from him in rebuke and correction, I perceived as hate and scorn. I knew it wasn't the right way. Other church members that knew about our family situation never bothered to reach out or showed a desire to help. I was hurting, mentally and emotionally, and all I could do was run.

CHAPTER 4
SO, WHAT HAPPENED?

The moments of resentment layered, one on top of the other. I felt myself drifting into the same footsteps as my mother: abandoning her first child, slipping into addictions, and dropping out of school at the age of 14. She had both sexual and heavy drug addictions. By the time my mother was 21, she had been incarcerated four times and had had two years of juvenile training school. I honestly loved my mother, but everyone around me hated her. I didn't know her well enough to hate her, but her actions made me battle my position.

From when I was seven until I was around fourteen years-old, we would come home from church and finding our house missing appliances, video games, TVs (How do you steal a heavy floor model TV anyway?), money, or jewelry.

I was taunted by my mother's actions. Others would shake their head at me, with shame. She would break into our neighbors' homes and steal everything she could grab. Everyone knew it was her! Addictions don't care who they hurt. Addictions have no respect. I hated her, but I loved her even more.

Following in her footsteps was painfully natural and easy. I had my first child and wasn't ready to take responsibility, so I left. I started going from house to house, staying wherever. I was broken and couldn't imagine being repaired. I needed answers that I felt only the streets could answer. I hung out with older guys from the hood, watching them and learning how and why they worked. These guys sold major weight. Some just did it to survive and provide through the struggle. The life of the ghetto was constantly at war with the my upbringing of living by faith, that would fill the gaps as we went from and paycheck to paycheck. I began to understand why felons sold drugs. It's not that I agreed, but I saw what limitations could do to a man's potential.

After hanging in the hood for months and never copping a bag, I was tired of watching other guys, and I was ready to do me: to start selling drugs. I did not even halfway know what I was doing. I had to learn the game from scratch and learn the street code. I was new to the game. Selling drugs was a big change for me. It changed my attitude, my respect, my relationship with my family, and the way I carried myself. I had no dignity. I was reckless, and I was knee-deep into it, but on the inside I was an insecure kid looking for validation in a cold world that wouldn't love me back.

CHAPTER 5
IT'S OVER

I was a sucker for the love of the game. I desperately needed validation. I was hanging with the wrong crowds, and I knew it. I had friends committing crazy crimes and getting life sentences, but we just carried on like it was nothing. I was eating with savages and didn't care. I was broken; like a deadly accident or like a wound that healed, and yet the scar remains to remind me it happened.

Rule #1: do not chase the money. Respect the game because the game does not respect you.

If anybody had the guts to stop me, that day in November 2005 would have been it. I was standing there in a stranger's backyard with my black ski mask and a black and white army camouflage jacket. My hands were numb and sweaty. The dude

I was with was excited as if he lived for this moment. I'm thinking to myself, 'Am I missing something? Was there another street code that I forgot?'

We both paced back and forth while rehearsing the plan. My mind drifted to a place where freedom had no limits. My adrenaline was bouncing off the walls, but that didn't stop me from what I came to do. It's amazing to me how fear will push you and what it can hinder you from doing. That night, it pushed me up a flight of stairs and into the back door of this drug dealer's apartment.

We entered the apartment late on a Friday night around 10:30 pm, intent on grabbing the excessive number of drugs and money that was there. I was anxious and scared. It was my first time being in this situation and, of course, I had no gun. I didn't even own one at the time. And from our inside tip, it was too sweet of a lick to need one. But we were told to watch our backs. Somewhere inside, there was a Mossberg pistol grip shotgun,.

We entered through the back door, which was ajar already. That was a red flag for me. After getting through the threshold of the back door, it was so dark I couldn't even see right in front of me. After noticing nothing was in place, as we were told, we backed out and decided to come back the next day.

CHAPTER 6
DAY TWO

We met up that morning. I felt eerie about the whole ordeal, but I had come that far, and there was no turning back now. We approached the house in broad daylight. It was roughly 9 am, and I was about to do one of the craziest things I'd ever do. I was standing ski-masked-up, knocking on the door.

"Who is it?" asked the guy on the other side of the door. If I ever was going to pee in my pants, this was it. We didn't respond. He opened the door. My partner in crime pushed through the doorway and I squeezed between them walking into the house. Things happened like a flash. I remember grabbing car keys, phones, and seeing his mother there like it was yesterday.

"Where's the gun?" I asked her.

"I don't know, sir!" She shrugged her shoulders in uncertainty, only to look in the direction of a closet. I opened the closet door, searching the back to find a black Mossberg pistol grip shotgun. I could hear small chatter in the back room.

"Where's it at?!" repeatedly asked my partner. In my head, the clock was ticking and my heartbeat could be felt in my hands. I was ready to go. My adrenaline was pumping faster. The apartment we were in was small, and everything felt intense.

At the most random moment, I heard a loud gunshot. My eardrums rung. It felt like I had been shot. As I turned and looked, I saw the victim bleeding from his inner thigh. It was loud in the room. I could feel the pain. I had never seen someone get shot before. Watching movies and hearing old war stories could have never built me for this moment.

He was laying there and bleeding badly. We got what we came for. The back door was 15 ft. away and I could not have been readier to go. Over the loudness of the television, I heard two names: one was Black, and the other was Chris.

"Yo, Chris! You! Let's go!"

Why did he say my name?! I thought that was why we had ski masks on; to hide our identity. We make a break for the door.

Eight months later, I pled guilty to armed robbery and assault with a deadly weapon. I was sentenced to 72 months in the state penitentiary. I couldn't believe what I was hearing, long hours and days, pending cases, and decisions, only to come down to this.

I sat in that courtroom, asking myself, "What just happened? What if I had another chance-- just one more shot?"

There were no second chances, no do-overs-- this was it. I was going to a place I had never been, but had only heard of. A place where I heard that you never want to go unless you care less about your life. A place where time stands still-- a land of the forgotten.

CHAPTER 7
NOBODY CRIES IN HERE

24 months prior, my mother was sentenced to another eight years and two months. Hearing the Judge give my sentence was painful. I could only imagine her pain. I'll never forget the long, sad walk of shame as I brutally took a last look at some of my family. To see the hurt and unexplainable pain that my grandmother was in. That was the moment I understood when she would say, "I love you so much. You're killing me!"

My life flashed before my eyes. I walked with my head down in shame, hurt, and rejection. It was all my fault. My grandmother screamed in that courtroom, "Chris!" My bones shook with regret that a new life was forming for her, and it was one that was being forced, not asked. She was the victim of a crime she didn't commit. She was crying over an incident she had nothing to do with. At that moment, I understood what true love was. Love covers all wrong, no matter what happened, love has a way of forgiving the unforgivable.

She moaned loudly. The bailiff assisted her, but she refused it. "Chris!" I couldn't look back this time. My legs were heavy. My tears wouldn't come pass my eyelids. The Judge yelled "Silence!" The way he hit the gavel felt as if nobody is allowed to cry in there. As he hit the gavel, my soul left me, feeling the cold, steel handcuffs placed on my wrists.

I walked into the holding cell. The bailiff whispered six words to me: "Never let them see you cry." I kept my head up. It was time to face reality. I made one phone call. I hung up the phone, with the new understanding that I had one thing to do, and that was to serve this time and come home. I was in a place where nobody cried, but I needed too.

CHAPTER 8
SERVING TIME

March 16, 2007 was the day I was sentenced to prison.

Prison changed me in ways I wish it hadn't.

Six years of my life were lost. After jail time and bail, I served five years and two months in prison. And if you're wondering what is bail? Bail is a temporary release of a prisoner in exchange for freedom. If a charge is pending against you, innocent or guilty, instead of sitting in jail until your court date, you have the option to pay the courts a retainer's fee in exchange for freedom. If you don't come to court for the charge against you, you've given up your rights for freedom.

The wounds, scars, and bruises are real, but now I'm healed and live to tell the story. I knew nothing about prison had no idea what to expect. I was blind to the fact that the next six years of my life would be changed forever. I no longer had the freedom I once had. I was now in controlled confinements and dictated permissions. Limited access was my demise. It was a world within a world, and life on the outside would not understand.

During my first six to eight months, I called home just about every day. Of course, I was homesick. Prison was full of AIDS, STDs, murderers, rapists, drug-dealers, thieves, and con artists. I found it surprising that this prison system expects you to change for the better regardless of your environment. I was surrounded by the lowest of society yet striving to be better and co-exist in the midst of chaos. All I could do was focus on finishing out my sentence.

Prison was another life-- the things that I heard, the things that I saw. Some things I wish I could forget, but yet are scarred into my memory. My emotions were a whirlwind. I wanted to go home. In my head, I kept apologizing. To what? To who? I had no idea. I needed to leave. This place was not for me. I used to talk my way out of trouble, but this time it was different. I felt trapped in my lies, and my environment was the truth that exposed it.

I walked into my first camp. Camp is what we said when referring to prison Each prisoner was recognized by the area code of your hometown. Which meant that I'm was now being associated with individuals I hadn't ever met. Only because we came from the same area code. Prison was different from what I expected it to be, far from the dramatic scenes I had seen while watching prison shows on National Geographic: the dark, gloomy feel, cave look, and nasty prison bars. As I was getting this tour, I noticed that it wasn't bad, but it definitely wasn't home.

What did it look like to serve time? It was cold, lonely, and bitter. Have you ever had headphones in your ears playing loud music, and someone was calling your name? No matter how loud anyone said your name, you still couldn't hear them.

Your awareness of your surroundings was lowered, and you were unaware of anything happening or changing around you. Your senses were numb to your surroundings.

That's how prison can be at times. We would listen to music to escape the pain of being in a place that feels cold, lonely, angry and bitter. No matter how many people you were around, none of them were there for you.

In prison, I learned the true meaning of time. We can't change time. We can't speed it up or slow it down. The only way to serve time is to have patience and a content understanding that 'I can't change my surroundings or circumstances, but I need my environment to give me purpose while I'm here.'

Serving time was challenging. It wasn't meant to be easy, I knew that. To be stripped from family and friends all at once was tough. I can only imagine what my ancestors went through to some degree-- being torn away from loved ones, never to see their children again.

Pain can be defined in two ways: to gain or to lose. The day I left to go to prison, I could barely tell you anything about me or who I really was. I was lost and confused and seeking validation to be accepted.

CHAPTER 9
BROKEN

A year flew by. Staying to myself was the smartest idea. From all the things that I'd seen and heard while learning to adapt, keeping to myself was the best teacher. Prison is a place of observation, not just participation. Being in prison built a wall within me to distrust people. I thought I knew or was well acquainted with liars, hustlers, manipulators, and honestly to sum it up, people who just didn't care. But in prison, people seemed to live like they had sold their soul. Hanging around each other for long enough led you the conclusion that you needed to just stay low key.

Something broke off in my soul. I became more and more distant than I knew was possible.

I squandered my money that my family had sent. I smoked weed. I drank. Whatever I could find to do, I did, just to escape the thought that I was out of sight and out of mind, and to escape the thought that no one cared.

CHAPTER 10
COUNT TIME

Every day we were counted like mules; nine times a day - the prison guards were always counting. In prison there's never a private moment. I used to hear people always say they strip you of your freedom, and that's true, but they forgot to mention one thing, the most important thing: they strip your inner peace.

At least in college, you have or had time alone. In prison, you don't. There are no doors in prison. Everything is open from the bathroom stalls to the showers; it's all open. The knowing of being watched used to bother me so badly. My inner peace was crushed.

They make you strip down before other officers, bend over and cough; making you feel belittled. Prison takes your manhood or what you thought made you who you are, and crushes it.

And yet I found hope that it wasn't forever. I lived nervously with the anticipation that something would happen to me. Something crazy happens every day in prison. It was hell and chaotic.

In prison you're two thoughts away from being in a psych-ward. The things you hear, see, and say can push you to your mind's greatest limits. Staying to yourself is the safest way to be.

CHAPTER 11
WHAT'S PRISON LIKE?

Some say the institution of prison used to be the institution of slavery and I can understand that to be true. These institution's profit in prisoners working for 70 cents a day or being forced to do manual labor every day, until the end of our sentencing. Can you imagine working 8 hours a day, 40 hours a week, to get paid $3.50 for the week?

To me personally, it's not about the money, and it's not about the labor. In my view, the American prison institution is continuing to develop poverty mindsets in inmates. The mentality that it produces is that 'I never have enough, and this is my worth.' All that's offered at the rate of crime is three meals and a cot. What is stripped from you is not only your liberty to travel or explore the world at any given moment, but also your financial freedom. The opportunity to get ahead in life and make better choices for your future financially becomes difficult. "Look at Norway's prison system and why it's so successful. Norway's incarceration rate just 75 per 100,000 people, compared to 707 people for every 100,000 people in the US. On top of that, when criminals in Norway leave prison they stay out. It has one of the lowest recidivism rates in the world at 22%." ("Why Norway Prison is Successful," Business Insider, 28 Nov 2017) Therefore, with that struggle, many inmates develop in the opposite direction, while being institutionalized into the system.

Prison can be compared to so many things. I liken it to a waiting room lobby. A place of expectation, a place to hear your name being called or news about what's next. A place where strangers meet and have one common goal: to serve time and go home. It has great limitations. You can't go far.

Anytime you're in a place you don't want to be, and others are there, it forces you to build relationships. While serving time, building connections with others helps distract you from time. It gets your mind off where you are for a while. You do not have to deal with reality.

My first 18 months flew by in prison. After accomplishing absolutely nothing to change for the better, I felt like I was done trying to prove to strangers that I was somebody. I was done trying to prove that I wasn't defined by the color of my prison jumpsuit. I was done trying to prove that I did have a good life and that I will go back to it. I put all of that aside, and instead I smoked, drank, played cards for money and food to survive. I stopped living like what I was trying to prove something.

I laughed out of pain. I wanted company because I was lonely.

I was broken. I needed help. In prison, there's a stigma of staying strong and never letting anyone see you cry. Pride wins in the face of hopelessness, addictions, sexual perversion, and any form of bondage you can imagine.

Prison was for the birds. This was going to be my first and last trip to this place. I was ready to make any changes needed to redirect the course in which I was headed. I needed help to heal and move on.

But just as in my childhood, I needed validation that I am somebody. I would walk into a dorm room facility where they housed inmates like cattle, and the only thing on my clothing that was of any worth was a bar code that read my I.D. number. That number held your whole identity as individual, your background, your strengths, inner circles, and known associations. Oftentimes, you were called by your "opus number."

It was a cool Saturday midafternoon. I was lying back, nodding off when I heard him.

"BOLDER."

"Yeah?" I yelled back at Sergeant, shocked to hear my actual name. "You've got a visitor," he said.

I quickly gathered myself, brushed my teeth, and greased down my hair. Walking towards the visitation entrance, all I could do was wonder who was waiting for me. My mind began to drift back, pondering what my life would be like if I hadn't gotten into any trouble. What if drugs, addictions, and wrong crowds never played a part in my life? Would I be here or be here by another unknown circumstance?

I believe every man and woman is dealt a hand in life, and it's their call to decide what to do with that hand. Whether you fold now or play it, you'll have to live with the choices you make.

CHAPTER 12
2008

"Hey momma," I said as I saw my grandmother sitting in the visitation room. My grandma would travel to the innermost parts of the jungle to see me no matter how far away from home I was. She was my ride or die. She would pop in at times, even when I didn't call home as much. At this visit, being incarcerated was really starting to kick in. Family visits lasted only for two hours and were limited to once a week, no matter how far your family had to travel to see you. They only got two hours.

Visits humbled you, in a different way. Seeing your family always brought you back to the reality that life is too short for mistakes and stupidity. One of the worst things I hated about family visits, and I'm sure I speak for all who've experienced this is seeing your loved ones walk away.

You cannot provide for your family or call home on the phone to hear their struggles and there's absolutely nothing you can do about it... that humbles you. Those moments remind you that being a street thug, gangster, or proving your manhood to so-called friends isn't worth it after all.

I hate that I had to go to prison to finally realize that this life wasn't it. Any good parent would want the best for their child, but there comes a time and season where every child must learn from what they've been taught. I played from the hand that was dealt for me and now, this time, I was done.

Prison is a correctional institution.

Okay, here's prison 101:

"Prisons have four major purposes. These purposes are retribution, incapacitation, deterrence and rehabilitation. Retribution means punishment for crimes against society. It means depriving you of your freedom as a way of making you pay a debt to society for your crime. Incapacitation refers to the removal of a person from society so that they can no longer harm innocent people. Deterrence means the prevention of future crime. It is hoped that prisons "provide warnings" to people thinking about committing crimes and that the possibility of going to prison will discourage people from breaking the law. Lastly, rehabilitation refers to activities designed to change you into law abiding citizens. These activities may include educational courses, learning job skills or counseling with a psychologist or social worker". [1]

The four primary purposes of prisons have not been stressed equally through the years. Still, society continues to tell the community that the system they have created works. Yet I still see young men and women going in and out of the prison system with no true rehabilitation.

It's not that going to prison means your life is over, or it's not worth still fighting for your future, but how you respond to life makes all the difference.

---

[1] (http://www.stoptheaca.org/purpose.html)

June of 2008 hit different for me than any other time since being in prison. I was tired of the life I had been living. It seemed like I couldn't freely break from the addictions I was in. I needed help, but I knew no one with an answer. The system designed to help me rehabilitate felt as if it were turning me into my worst. There was no saving me, no help, and no light at the end of the tunnel.

I was in a rigged system. Instead of evolving into a better member that could contribute to society, I found myself bound to addiction. It was easy to get in, and horribly tough to get out. To think one could escape a mental place like that was a laugh within itself. This was a place where men glorified masturbation and porn, and where they idolized random, nude pictures of women that represented a fantasy and filled a dark void. This was a place where they continued to commit the same petty crimes that got them in there in the first place, but they turned the other cheek like it's some street code of honor. And every day, I watched a man walk out the front gates and back into society with a wounded heart and mental dysfunction. I would hear them chant, "I'm free!" But I knew that wasn't freedom, that's a trap. I knew before leaving, I was going to need true freedom. Not just from addictions and drugs, but something greater had to change.

The summer days of 2008 in prison weren't too bad, but it depended on which camp you were at because some had no air conditioning.

That Saturday night was so hot that I couldn't sleep. I was tossing and turning. My heart was heavy. I prayed; I tried talking to God throughout the night... no response. I felt like the walls were closing in on me. The flashbacks of November 2005 haunted me with regrets that no forgiveness or healing could fill my void.

Daylight broke through the window, barely past my locker and bunk bed railing. I sat there on the edge of my bed as sweat dripped from my face to the floor. I held my head down in my hands and elbows on my knees. There was one question I kept reciting in my head for three hours. "Is God real?"

I needed answers, but not just answers for head knowledge; I needed proof. Everybody has an answer, until it's time to prove it. I'm what you would call a risk taker. I don't believe in what data says or theory. I'm a firm believer that possibilities belong to the one who tries their faith.

I got up from the bed went to a seemingly random church service, because I was hungry for answers. The service was good. The sermon was okay. I mean, I grew up in the church. Nothing was different besides my location. The preacher offered salvation. I hesitated. I was telling myself, 'I've been here before. What is the difference?' The difference was that I wasn't looking for a religion but a relationship. I accepted Christ that day in June of 2008.

CHAPTER 13
RELATIONSHIP > RELIGION

Do you ever feel like you were still missing something, after receiving the very thing you've been looking for? Well, that was me after receiving Christ. I'll be honest; I still felt the same. There was no parade or lights, no early release from prison. But that wasn't important to me. I just wanted intimacy with God.

I sat on my bed in silence that night. Suddenly, I broke it by stating something to God. I said, "God, if you're as real as my family talks about, if you're as true as my grandmother shouted and preached about for years, now is a dope time to prove it. Are you the God of my strength and weakness? I don't want to get to know a God of pages, but the God of the ages. I want to experience You like never before." I decided to put the relationship to the test. I told God, "If you can deliver me from smoking, then I promise you I'll serve you until I die. I won't give up. It may not be perfect, but I'm all-in."

That Monday morning, something hit differently. I woke up gagging at the hint of secondhand smoke. Another prisoner was trying to sneak a smoke before being seen by a guard. I was choking.

"Bro, you good?" he questioned as I coughed. I couldn't breathe. My eyes were watering. He asked me, "Don't you smoke, man?" That's when it hit me! "Nah, I don't anymore," I replied.

I couldn't believe it! I felt as if I had never smoked before. I know it sounds crazy that the night before, I was telling God, 'if you deliver me from smoking, I'll serve you,' and exactly the next morning... we've got a choker?! That was healing power! That was the God I needed to meet, and that was what I needed to see. I didn't need to meet the 'wing it off with nicotine' God. I needed and experienced the hand of God. He met me right there. He came in and felt the need to touch me.

I was introduced to a relationship that is greater than any religion. This encounter reminded me of the Isaiah-effect in the bible, in the book of Isaiah chapter 6 verses 1-10 you'll read that the prophet saw a vision and wanted to accept the call but was feeling unworthy because of the foulness of his mouth. So, the Angel touched his mouth that it may be pure. God desires to have relationships, not checklists. I knew if this was going to be done. I had to be solid in my transformation with Christ.

I didn't have all my ducks in a row, yet I was entirely sure about this walk, and I wanted to be faithful. I began cutting things out of my life that didn't help or better my character. The next act of faith was dealing with the people I was hanging around. At first, I didn't notice the impact they had on me until one day in prayer, I asked God why I still struggled with cursing, and He showed me: the influence of my friends.

A true test of my character and walk was the moment I decided I wasn't hanging around the people who validated me. That was the moment I began to be tested like never before. I got called every hypocritical name you could think. I was shunned. Circles I once was invited to be a part of now huddled in a different place, I ate alone, walked alone, and I felt forced to stay to myself. If there's one thing worse than being in prison, serving time, and being away from family, it is feeling completely alone.

CHAPTER 14
EYES OPEN

A changed mind in prison is tougher than a changed heart in the free world!

I was living against the odds and playing the hand that was dealt to me. The transformation was like no other. My family didn't recognize me. Other inmates saw my passion. I was changing. I was beginning to live a life of urgency, not complacency; a life of determination and purpose, not religion. I was restoring the hope of a second chance. I wanted my hood to see new hope. I wanted them to see somebody they knew and could relate to undergo an undeniable change so that they couldn't deny the power of God.

I fellowshipped with Muslims and Mormons. I studied with Moor Science, Rasa, Black Hebrews, and more. I mean,

Jehovah's Witnesses always ran me off, but we still kicked it. I never discredited anyone's faith. I let the truth do that.

I enjoyed studying with other faiths and beliefs and finding common ground. That's love. I believe God created us all for a purpose, and the more I seek that truth, the closer I felt whole.

And then there was the dream...

Now, I am a dreamer on a normal night. But the vision on this night scared the heck out of me! It also ignited in me something that still burns in my soul.

In this dream, I woke up to men's screams throughout the camp. Men were everywhere, running wild, and screaming at the top of their lungs. At first, I covered my ears. Everything was on fire. The walls were engulfed in flames. Men were choking, suffocating, and passing out. I quickly got up and began walking to the outer door. I continued to pat myself, wondering why I wasn't on fire. I walked throughout the prison camp. I saw men that I knew burning. I noticed something else weird. Every time I as started to walk about, men were reaching out to me, reaching for my hand.

As I looked down at my left hand, I saw that I was carrying a water bottle with a label that read: Salvation. At that moment, the Lord spoke to me and said, "You carry the oil of water, that is needed to quench men's hearts, in your hands."

I opened the bottle and began splashing and throwing water on men as I ran throughout the camp, praying in the spirit. The men that received it got up.

That vision changed my life. I never read the Bible the same way after that. I never took for granted my encounters and experiences. God was doing a work in me, and I now understood the cost of what was at stake.

My personal time with God grew quickly. My studies increased from two hours a day to six to eight hours of intense study per day. I aimed to read thoroughly through the scriptures, not to be a pastor or teacher. Things I thought I was taught growing up in church, I began to learn for myself. I found that there was a lot of information that was miscommunicated, misinterpreted, and therefore, causing me to live altered. So, I made it my mission to learn and become very skilled. I studied towards new degrees and started taking other college courses while incarcerated. I became a mentor of spiritual freedom to others in the GED educational development course.

I hated seeing young men come to prison, wasting their potential, and the older men feeling like it's too late. Success isn't determined by age or gender; it's your passion to see yourself win.

CHAPTER 15
BLACK & WHITE

Sitting in a prison cell will make you reflect a lot. Sometimes I would think about my biological father. Would he write to me? Visit? Honestly, anything? What I would give some days to have a father pump my chest and say, "Chris, you got this," or grab me by the neck and lead me. I now fully understand how tough it can be to not have a father. I felt robbed of being a son. I could be called a grandson, a nephew, a cousin, but never truly a son.

I watched men leave prison, and sometimes within weeks they came back. I wanted to be sure that wouldn't happen to me. I remember sitting at Lexington Correctional, waiting to hear my name. The anticipation of going home after six years was breathtaking.

Don't get me wrong, prison became something to me when I began to make the best of my situation. I was one of the first inmates to be allowed to transfer camps, in order to share my testimony. I worked closely with the administration to help structure and detail staff and inmate relations. So, after six years, to me prison had become a temporary home.

On June 25, 2012, my name was called to go home for the first time in six years. The feeling was unexplainable. I couldn't process it. I was finally going home. I didn't know what to expect. I spent my first few days trying to get into a routine of things. Home felt normal. My life had changed, but the environment where I came from hadn't. The guys on the street corner were still doing the same old thing. Others were still in the same spot as they were when I left. Six years... yet no change. It started to bother me and then I remember telling myself, "Life is black & white. You get what's there. Life doesn't create opportunities-- you do."

Everything I learned over the years in prison came down to the moments of not making excuses for what I don't have but taking responsibility for what I have now. When I came home in

2012, I had no job, no driver's license, no car, no money, no connections, no clothes, and nowhere to start.

ALL I HAD WAS A PLAN. A plan is a seed, and when we plant our plans, they began to grow into trees. Now, storms and unconditional weather pulls at our trees, but it's all a part of the enduring process for the trees to grow stronger. Your plans are tested against hardships and challenges. That's what going home was like. It was challenging but worth it.

What changed? Just my mentality. That's what changed. The likelihood of coming home to the same environment then returning to being incarcerated is 87%, but something had changed for me. My system was different. I rooted myself in the system of Jesus Christ. I didn't just read the Bible, I got it in me. I didn't just try Jesus out for a chance, I gave Him my life.

I lived to show that my mentality was fixed, on purpose. I was no longer seeking attention or playing the victim. I used my weakness for strength.

CHAPTER 16
BROKEN

In 2012, I got married. The following year, I planted a church. Our first church plant was trial and error, but we learned. We weren't taught how to do things, but we tried, and God provided. We planted our church without a team, as a first-time pastor I didn't even know what I was getting into. There were two things I knew I could do well. One was to pray and two was to encourage others. Unfortunately, that's not enough to plant a church, but enough for us to trust God to lead. In the meantime, my wife and I were still thankful for the souls that received Christ and the hearts that were transformed. Even though we had no clue what we were doing, we knew we heard God. I learned that faith will convince you to do some crazy things. Four years and three kids later, I heard God say that it was time to plant another church. Even though I and the people around me had no idea what we were doing, all I knew that God had called me and that the vision of the fire in the prison still haunted me.

I'm thankful to be where I am. God protected me over the years. My past is tough and I can admit that, but it seems like God's grace is greater.

Being born to a mother who didn't want me and to a father who turned his back on me is more than adversity. I often still feel their abandonment, but because God's love covers me, I'm able to heal through the lens of forgiveness. My grandmother was my sacrifice. What she has done for me, I will never be able to repay or forget. I couldn't write enough to tell it all.

I think back on how foolish I was to commit a crime that not only separated us but broke her heart. I still have flashbacks about that night. I had never seen someone get shot up close before. Everything was fast and sometimes faster.

Sometimes I reflect, thinking over how everything happens for a purpose. No matter your circumstance or situation, there's a greater lesson to learn and grow from. I needed healing for many years. I was the only one who served any time for the crime, but I needed to see consequences for my mistakes, and I needed to develop into my purpose. Without that, it would have been very difficult to fulfill my purpose, that God had for me. I would have found it difficult to form relationships and connections would have been ruined if I had not sat in a place to wait, hear from God, develop, and become better.

Coming from a broken place isn't meant to destroy you. It is meant to remind you that you're not in control.

BROKEN: damaged or altered by or as if by breaking

When we live by how the world defines us, often we end up in places and circumstances that measure out to the name that we've accepted. But we aren't broken, as the world sees us. We're healed as Christ has declared us.

Jeremiah 29:11 says, "For I know the thoughts that I think toward you, thoughts of peace, and not of evil, to give you an expected end."

I have realized that I don't have to live in brokenness because there's an expected end for me. Knowing that brings me greater peace because my beginning didn't seem to be expected, nor was it peaceful. Today, I strive to continue to be an example in and throughout my community. I continue to mentor men and help strengthen families. My passion is to plant churches and develop training centers around the nation where men, women, and youth can receive spiritual guidance, educational and fundamental development for employment, and other practical purposes. I seek to see our community changed, restored, and filled with purpose.

Your dreams need rest. Your visions need faith, and your plans are seeds that need to be planted to grow. Prepare for adversity and let your discipline be greater than your motivation.

Peace.

ABOUT THE AUTHOR

Christopher Bolder is a dynamic speaker, coach and leader within the community. Upon his reentry back into society, he holds 2 degrees for Psychological and family counseling to help returning citizens successfully "reenter" society following their incarceration, thereby reducing recidivism.

Chris is the founder of Bolder Faith an organization that coaches you to live a better life.

Chris is currently a Pastor of a thriving church in Charlotte, NC and he and his wife Brittney have 3 beautiful children.

Made in the USA
Monee, IL
04 June 2021

69375147R00039